Contents

Spiders

With their long legs, hairy bodies and elaborate webs, spiders are intriguing creatures. Despite having a fearsome reputation, most cannot harm humans and some spiders are interesting to look after as pets.

Arachnids

Spiders belong to a group of animals called arachnids, which also includes scorpions, ticks and mites. Arachnids are small creatures with segmented bodies protected by an external skeleton (exoskeleton) made of tough skin. They are cold-blooded, which means that their body temperature varies with the temperature of their surroundings.

Spider parts

A spider's body has two parts – the cephalothorax, or head section, and the abdomen. Attached to the cephalothorax are eight legs, and a pair of pedipalps. These look like shorter legs and help the spider to pick up smells and catch prey. Also attached to the head section are the chelicerae. These are the spider's mouth parts and contain its fangs. Most spiders have four pairs of eyes, situated on the top of the cephalothorax. The abdomen contains many of the spider's organs, such as the heart, stomach and lungs.

Hairy bodies

Most spiders are covered with long hairs. These hairs are very sensitive to movement, heat, and other triggers in a spider's surroundings. Through these hairs spiders can feel tiny vibrations, helping them to locate prey and detect danger. It is just as well, as the eyesight of many types of spider is quite poor.

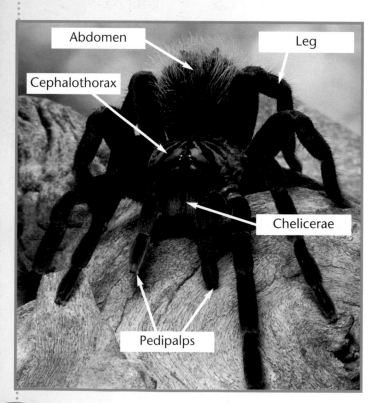

Abdomen

Leg

Cephalothorax

Chelicerae

Pedipalps

Spiders have segmented bodies that are covered in hair, and eight legs that are attached to the cephalothorax.

...Exotic Pets...

SPIDER

Selina Wood

W
FRANKLIN WATTS
LONDON • SYDNEY

This edition 2010.

First published in 2007 by Franklin Watts
338 Euston Road, London NW1 3BH

Franklin Watts Australia
Level 17/207 Kent Street
Sydney NSW 2000

Editor: Rachel Tonkin and Julia Bird
Designer: Proof Books
Picture researcher: Diana Morris

Picture credits: Alinari/Topfoto: 6; Gregory Basco/Deep Green
Photography/PD: 28; James Carmichael Jr/NHPA: 4; Corbis: 10;
Rose Di Biasi/Freezepic Photography/PD: 22; Mark
Fairhurst/UPPA/Topfoto: 17; Robert Kwaka: 12, 29;
Robert Kwaka/PD: front cover, 1, 9, 18, 26; Jean Preston-
Mafham/Premaphoto/PD: 25; Bill Morgenstern/Earth Moods
Photography/PD: 24; Rob & Ann Simpson/Sargent Stock Image
Resource/PD: 8; Stefan Sollfars/PD: 7; Kim Taylor/Nature PL: 11.
Francesco Tomasinelli/Natural Visions: 13; Wegner/Arco/Nature PL: 5.

With thanks to Mitch and Hazel Price at The Reptile Experience.

A CIP catalogue record for this book
is available from the British Library

ISBN: 978 0 7496 9675 7
Dewey Classification: 639'.7

Printed in China

Franklin Watts is a division of Hachette Children's Books,
an Hachette Livre UK company.
www.hachette.co.uk

Expert spinners

All spiders have special glands that produce silk. Silk is made in a spider's abdomen and then drawn out through tube-shaped organs at the back of its body called spinnerets. Spiders use silk for a variety of different tasks – making webs to trap prey, building nests and protecting their eggs, as well as communicating with other spiders. Most spiders spin a thread of silk behind them wherever they go. Small spiders can travel great distances, even as far as hundreds of kilometres, floating along on a drag line of silk.

Spiders' webs come in different shapes and sizes depending on the species of spider that has made it. Webs can be flat like a sheet or shaped like a funnel, but the most common is the spiral web, built by orb spiders.

Liquid silk is produced in a spider's abdomen and comes out through its spinnerets.

Steely silk

Silk is one of the strongest fibres in the natural world. It is six times stronger than steel of the same weight.

Fast movers

Spiders have eight legs, so they can move quickly around obstacles. At the end of each leg are two clingy claws that help a spider climb up smooth and steep surfaces. Spiders rely on blood pressure to straighten their legs and walk. If they do not have enough fluid in their body, their blood pressure drops. Their legs curl up beneath them and they cannot walk.

Questions & Answers

✴ **Do spiders have blood?**
Yes, but it is not red, it is pale blue. Spiders do not have blood vessels. Instead, the blood runs freely around the organs inside their body.

✴ **Do spiders have brains?**
Spiders have a mass of nerve tissue near their eyes where they pick up information from their sense organs. This works like a primitive brain.

✴ **How do spiders reproduce?**
After mating with a male spider, female spiders lay eggs in a cocoon of silk. Some species look after the eggs until they hatch, and a few types actually help their babies (spiderlings) to feed.

Spiders in the wild

There are over 36,000 known species of spider and they live all over the world, making homes almost anywhere, from gaps in floorboards to air bubbles in ponds.

Spider homes

Spiders thrive in many habitats including gardens, fields, tropical forests, deserts and mountains. Many live close to humans, in the nooks and crannies of buildings. The trapdoor spider lives in a burrow in the ground, with a hinged door made of silk, twigs and earth, waiting to ambush prey. Water spiders live in ponds. They trap bubbles of air in their silk web so that they can breathe underwater.

Orb spiders make their homes in fields and gardens all over the world.

Escaping predators

Spiders are mostly solitary animals that prefer to live on their own, only coming together briefly to mate. They have many natural enemies in the wild – frogs, lizards and birds eat smaller spiders, and owls, large centipedes and large wasps hunt down bigger spiders, such as tarantulas. To escape, small spiders can swing away on their trap line silk (see page 7). Larger spiders may run away and hide, or as a last resort, bite with their fangs.

Well disguised

Brown and black is the predominant colouring of spiders. These colours help them to blend in with their surroundings and hide from both predators and prey. A species called crab spiders can even change their colouring to suit their environment. They prey on insects and hide in flowers, changing colour to match their background and stop their prey from spotting them.

Predators

Spiders use their fangs to inject venom that paralyses their prey, which are usually insects, such as flies. Some, such as the jumping spider, stalk and then pounce on their prey, while others build webs or traps to capture their food. Once the prey is trapped, the spider wraps it in silk to stop it escaping. It then dribbles digestive juices onto its prey, which turns it into a gooey substance that the spider can suck up into its mouth. Spiders do not like to eat animals that are already dead.

This Cross spider has wrapped its prey in silk and is using its fangs to devour it.

Girl power

Most female spiders are larger and stronger than male spiders and occasionally even eat the males after mating!

Trap lines

Tarantulas, the largest species of spiders, do not use webs to trap their prey. Instead, some tarantulas spin a series of fine trap lines outside their burrow. One end of each line is attached to the spider's nest. The spider can feel when prey is touching a line, and rushes out to capture it. Other types of tarantula simply lie in wait and then run down their prey.

Questions & Answers

✳ **How big can a spider's prey be?**
Large spiders, such as tarantulas, can tackle frogs, lizards, mice and even small birds.

✳ **How long do spiders live?**
Most spiders live for about a year, but larger species can live for more than 20 years. Many male spiders die soon after mating.

✳ **How does venom kill?**
Some types of venom affect the nervous system of prey, stopping the heart and lungs from working, and paralysing muscles. Other types damage blood vessels and body tissue.

Spiders as pets

Spiders are unique creatures that can make fascinating pets, but it is important to check out all the facts before you decide to keep one in your home. Spiders require special care and only a few types thrive as pets.

Choose carefully

Some highly venomous spiders, such as Black Widows or Sydney Funnel Webs, are very dangerous and should definitely be left to the experts. It is also not a good idea to take spiders from the wild, even if they are harmless. You may not be able to find out what they need to stay alive and they may also be more prone to diseases. Moreover, it is illegal in some countries to take animals from the wild.

The Black Widow spider, easily recognised by its red markings, has very poisonous venom and should never be kept as a pet.

A spider's needs

Remember you will have to provide food, shelter and health care for your pet spider throughout its life. Find out how long your spider is likely to live and how much it will cost to look after it. Also remember that spiders and other pets such as dogs and cats don't mix well.

Tarantulas as pets

Many people choose to keep tarantulas as pets. Large and exotic looking, these spiders from the tropics are interesting to keep. There are two types of tarantula – ground-dwellers and arboreal tarantulas that live in trees in the wild. The ground-dwelling tarantulas are easier to look after. Some species of tarantula are too aggressive to make good pets, so make sure you do lots of research into different species before you buy one.

Bitter bite

Nearly all spiders are venomous, but only around 25 species have venom strong enough to seriously harm a human.

The right pet for you?

Spiders are very quiet animals. They do not take up too much room, and do not need to be taken for walks. Their tanks (see page 14–15) are quite easy to keep clean, too. Remember, however, they can bite when frightened, and they are not cuddly – they are for watching rather than touching. Spiders also need a diet of live insects!

Questions & Answers

✱ **What is CITES?**
The Convention on International Trade in Endangered Species is an agreement between international governments. Its aim is to ensure that trade in wild animals and plants does not threaten their survival.

✱ **Will I need a permit to keep a spider?**
For some endangered or more dangerous types you may need a permit. Always check with your local government authority to see whether you need a license to keep the spider that you want.

Endangered spiders

Some types of spider are endangered in the wild due to habitat destruction, and because large numbers have been collected to be sold in the pet trade. Now some of these animals, such as the Mexican Red Knee tarantula, are protected under the Convention on International Trade in Endangered Species (CITES). Only Red Knees that have been bred in captivity can be bought and sold.

Mexican Red Knee tarantulas are popular pets with very distinctive markings.

Pet research

Before you buy a spider as a pet, find out all you can about spiders from the Internet, books and magazines, national arachnid societies and animal welfare organisations (see page 31 for some suggestions). Ask people you know who already keep spiders for their advice and tips on how to care for a pet spider.

Tarantula types

There are many types of tarantula available through the pet trade, but if you have never owned one before, it is best to begin with a docile, easy-going species that is relatively straightforward to look after.

Ones to pick

Opt for an American, ground-dwelling tarantula as these are usually less aggressive than African or Asian tarantulas. However, American tarantulas have barbed hairs on their abdomen, known as urticating hairs, that they kick off when threatened. These hairs can make human skin come out in a rash and are particularly irritating to the eye. Make sure you wash your hands after handling your spider or cleaning out its tank.

The Chilean Rose is an attractive, calm spider with a brown body covered with pinkish hairs.

Chilean Rose
(Grammostola rosea)

A Chilean Rose is a good tarantula for a beginner. It is a docile, hardy, ground-dwelling spider that comes from the foothills of the Andes mountains in South America. It is a medium-sized spider, reaching a leg span of 10cm. It prefers slightly humid conditions but can also live in a dryer tank, and prefers a temperature range of 22–30°C.

Curly Hair
(Brachypelma albopilosa)

The Curly Hair tarantula is dark brown with long, curly, light brown hairs scattered over its body and legs. Its leg span can reach 12.5cm. It is native to Central America where it lives in burrows in the ground. It is docile and prefers fairly humid conditions. Females can live for over ten years, but males can die after just three or four years.

Mexican Red Rump
(Brachypelma vagans)

This handsome spider comes from Mexico and other parts of Central America. It has glossy black hairs, an orange edge along the front of its body and long reddish hairs on its abdomen. It prefers slightly more humid conditions and a stable temperature of about 23–27°C. Mexican Red Rumps' bodies can grow to 5–7.5cm, with a leg span up to 13.5cm. The females can live for up to 15 years, but males only survive for around two years.

The Mexican Red Rump likes to burrow and should be provided with lots of floor covering.

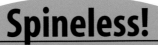

Spineless!

Tarantulas are among the largest land invertebrates (animals without backbones).

Mexican Red Knee
(Brachypelma smithi)

This beautiful spider has black and orange legs. Robust and docile, it is the most popular tarantula to keep as a pet, but it does have a tendency to kick off its hairs. Its body grows to about 5cm long and it has a leg span of about 12.5 cm. It requires a daytime temperature of around 24–30°C. Males live for about ten years, while females can live for up to 25 years.

Remember!

Whatever species of tarantula you decide to get, make sure you know about its specific needs before you buy it. Different tarantulas have slightly different care requirements and may suffer if kept in the wrong conditions.

Questions & Answers

✳ **Where does the name 'tarantula' come from?**
The name tarantula used to belong to the European Wolf Spider, which was named after the Italian town of Taranto where it lives. When European explorers first discovered the big, hairy spiders native to America which looked like tarantulas, they gave them the same name, despite the fact that they were not related to the European Wolf Spider, and the name stuck.

✳ **Should I buy a male or a female?**
Female tarantulas live much longer than males – twice as long or more.

✳ **Why do tarantulas moult?**
Tarantulas have to moult or shed their outer skeleton in order to grow. Most tarantulas shed more than 20 times in their lifetime.

Selecting your spider

Once you have found out all you can about tarantulas, your next step is to find a good specialist pet shop or tarantula breeder where you can buy all the right equipment and find a pet that suits you.

Where can I buy a tarantula?

You can find out about tarantula breeders and specialist pet shops on the Internet, and through your national tarantula society (see page 31). Sometimes these organisations hold shows where many types of tarantulas are on display to buy. You can also ask your local vet or national animal welfare organisation for advice. You should look for a reputable specialist pet shop or breeder that looks after its animals well, and cares about their future.

Do lots of research into the different species of tarantula before buying your pet, and choose it very carefully.

Spotting the right spider

There may be a large selection of spiders on offer at the shop or breeder. It is important to be clear about the species of the spider you are buying (find out its Latin or scientific name if possible) to avoid any confusion. Otherwise you may end up with more than you bargained for!

Captive-bred?

Ask for a spider that has been bred in captivity. Don't buy spiders that have been taken from the wild as this endangers natural populations. Captive-bred spiders of the Brachy-pelma species (which include the Mexican Red Knee and Curly Hair) are widely available, and are often sold as tiny babies or spiderlings.

Ask questions

Take your time choosing a spider at a pet shop or breeder. The tanks should look clean and the spiders healthy. Ask the breeder lots of questions. Find out about the spider's history, how old the spider is, what equipment it needs and what it likes to eat. The breeder should be able to answer all your questions.

Questions & Answers

* **Can I keep more than one spider in a tank?**
Spiders should always be housed alone as they will kill and even eat one another if put together.

* **Should I buy a young or an older spider?**
It's best to buy a spider that is young as it will find it easier to adjust to a new home and you are likely to get more information about its history.

* **How will I know what equipment I need?**
A good pet shop or breeder should be able to advise you on the sort of tank and equipment you need.

Buying spiderlings

Some captive-bred spiders are sold as spiderlings. There is quite a lot of information available on how to look after baby spiders as they grow up. However, it is not possible to tell the sex of tarantulas until they have reached adulthood.

Do not buy a spider if:

* it has mites or ticks on its body
* it has bumps or cuts
* it is huddled in a corner with its legs under its body
* it seems nervous or aggressive
* it has a bald abdomen due to flicking its hairs (see page 10).

Arachnophobia

The fear of spiders is called arachnophobia. It is one of the most common of all human phobias, or fears.

Tiny tarantula spiderlings can be kept together only when they are very young.

Creating a home

Setting up a home for your spider is quite simple and fun to do. Have all the main components ready so you can cause as little disturbance as possible to your pet when you bring it home.

Housing

There are several different types of containers suitable for housing tarantulas, but a small glass fish tank (30 x 20 x 15cm) is probably the best if you want to be able to watch your pet. You can also use plastic storage boxes. Make sure the lid is very secure (weigh it down if necessary) and seal up any gaps as tarantulas can escape surprisingly easily. The tank should have some small (2–4mm) ventilation holes. Put the tank somewhere stable where it can't be knocked over, out of direct sunlight, but somewhere fairly warm.

A ground-dwelling spider requires a simple home with plenty of substrate, a shelter and a water dish.

Beware!

Make sure your tank doesn't have any sharp edges, and avoid putting anything sharp into the tank where it could injure your delicate pet. Also make sure that there are no gaps where a spider can get its legs stuck.

Inside the tank

Cover the floor of the tank with material, known as substrate, to keep your spider comfortable and warm. Various types of substrate are available, but one of the easiest to get hold of is moss peat (without added fertilisers). It should be sterilised first because it may contain mites that could kill your spider. Ask an adult to put the peat in a microwave for ten minutes. After it has cooled down, place a 3–5cm layer across the bottom of the tank. Pour a little water on the substrate on one side of the tank to make it damp, but keep the other side dry.

Keeping it warm

The temperature of the tank should be kept close to that of the tarantula's natural habitat, so you will probably need to supply extra heating. The easiest way to do this is by placing a heating pad under the substrate across half of the tank (you can buy different heating pads in different sizes). As a cold-blooded animal whose temperature varies with its surroundings, a tarantula needs both a warm and a cool area to regulate its body temperature. The ideal temperature to keep tarantulas is between 22–30°C, but always check the special requirements of the species you are keeping. Below the lowest recommended temperature they become sluggish and may stop feeding. However, a tank that is too hot is also harmful.

Lighting

Nearly all tarantulas are nocturnal and spend daytime in their burrow or shelter. Therefore they don't like bright light. Do not place the tank near a window, where the sun's rays can make the tank too bright and hot, but do not place the tank in complete darkness either.

Questions & Answers

✳ How big should the tank be?
Tarantulas do not need a lot of space, but they should have enough room for a burrow or shelter, a water dish and space to walk a few paces. A 30 x 20 x 15cm tank is about right for most adult tarantulas.

✳ Is heating the tank important?
Yes, a spider can die if it gets too hot or too cold. You should check the temperature of different parts of the tank regularly with a thermometer. Alternatively, you can install a thermostat (available from good pet shops) in your tank.

✳ Can I use gravel or cat litter to cover the tank's floor?
No, these materials trap moisture and filth and can cause serious harm if they are eaten by the spider. Also avoid cedar wood shavings, as these can be poisonous to your pet.

Here is some of the equipment you will need to look after your spider: heating pad, bark piece (for shelter), thermostat, water dish, crickets (for food), tweezers or small scissors for handling food, a paintbrush for moving your spider around, and vitamin dust for nutrients.

Tank accessories

To keep your spider comfortable and healthy make sure the conditions of the tank are as near as possible to those your spider would experience in the wild. Set the tank up step by step.

Water bowl

All tarantulas, including those from desert habitats, need daily access to clean drinking water. In order to drink, a tarantula has to place its whole face in the water dish. Use a shallow dish that is heavy enough not to be tipped over. A plastic plant dish should be sufficient. For smaller spiders and spiderlings, you should use a shallower dish (e.g. a plastic lid) or add something to the water dish so that the spider can't fall in and drown whilst drinking.

A piece of sponge will prevent younger spiders from falling into their water dish.

Shelters

All tarantulas need a dark shelter where they can hide during daylight hours. You can make a shelter for your pet out of an old plastic plant pot, cut in half. Wood pieces make a good shelter, but can go mouldy. Sink the shelter into the substrate, making sure it is dark inside, with a small entrance for your spider to squeeze through. Your pet may make a few additions to the shelter itself. Don't be surprised if your pet spends hours or even days in there!

Humidity

It is important to have the right level of ventilation and humidity in the tank. You can keep it damp by spraying a little water on the substrate about once a week. Make sure that the tank has enough ventilation so that the air doesn't become too damp, as this can encourage mould.

Spiderlings

Baby food jars or small plastic tubs (eg margarine tubs) are ideal homes for spiderlings. Add a few ventilation holes and a layer of substrate. Spiderlings need a high level of humidity in the tank, as they suck the substrate to drink, so you should spray the tub every day. Make sure you keep your spiderlings somewhere warm until they are ready to be transferred to a bigger tank with a heating pad.

This young Mexican Red Knee tarantula is developing the colouring and hairs of an adult.

Hide and seek

If your spider is tucked away in its burrow most of the day, it is a sign that it's healthy and happy!

Rocks and branches

Tarantulas that live on the ground in the wild are happy with quite a simple tank, and don't need rocks and branches to climb on. In fact, they may injure themselves if they try to climb too high and fall, and even a minor fall can prove fatal to a tarantula. If you keep a tree-dwelling tarantula, it is a good idea to put some small tree branches in the tank. Make sure they have no sharp splinters and are free of mites before you introduce them to the tank.

Questions & Answers

✱ **How can I check the humidity level of my tank?**
You can buy something called a hygrometer, which measures humidity levels. These are available from good pet shops.

✱ **Can I add plants to the tank?**
A tarantula is usually happy with quite a plain tank with substrate, and adding plants may introduce disease and make the tank more difficult to clean.

✱ **Can I use fish tank ornaments to construct a shelter?**
It is best not to, as tarantulas can easily get stuck in these.

Feeding your pet

Feeding your spider can be one of the most exciting aspects of looking after it. It can be fascinating to watch a spider eat, but make sure you feed it the correct food to keep it healthy.

Feeding time

Tarantulas' main diet is live crickets but they will also eat locusts, grasshoppers and mealworms. You can buy these from specialist pet shops or breeders. Spiderlings should be fed fruit flies, pin-head crickets and freshly split crickets. Gently place the food near to where the tarantula normally moves around and your pet should find it.

How much?

Tarantulas prefer to eat food that is half their own body length or less. It is not easy to overfeed them as they will generally only eat as much food as they need. An average-sized adult tarantula needs to eat about four large crickets a week. You can feed these to your pet all in one go and it will not need feeding again for the rest of the week.

This Mexican Red Knee is poised to strike at its prey – a small beetle.

Live prey

Always remove live prey that isn't eaten as it may attack your spider. Moulting spiders (see page 21) are particularly vulnerable to attack from their prey. Spiders stop eating for a few weeks when they are moulting (a few days if they are spiderlings).

Tasty treats

For a change of routine, you may be able to persuade your spider to take dead food, such as small pieces of raw lean beef or thawed baby mice called pinkies (available from pet shops that specialise in reptiles). If necessary, use a piece of string or prongs to dangle and jostle the prey around to make it look as if it is alive.

Nasty food!

If you decide to feed your pet other insects besides crickets, always check that they won't harm your spider. Avoid feeding your spider some types of food such as earwigs. They can be poisonous to your pet.

Questions & Answers

* **What if my spider doesn't eat the food I've given it?**
Try a change of diet but remember that it is normal for a tarantula to be off its food before it moults and sometimes during the cooler, winter months. But if your pet still refuses food after a few weeks, seek expert advice.

* **Can I feed my spider insects I have found in the wild?**
It is best not to. They may have been exposed to pesticides or parasites that could harm your pet.

Fast food

In the wild, a large tarantula can reduce a mouse to a pile of bones and hair within 36 hours.

Leftovers

It is fascinating to watch a tarantula pounce on its prey and subdue it with its fangs. A tarantula has usually finished devouring its prey after 24 hours. You should take away the remains before they start to decay.

If your tarantula is refusing to eat for any reason, try tempting it with a pinkie.

Staying healthy

One of your main responsibilities as a tarantula owner is to keep your pet's tank clean. This should be easy once it becomes part of your care routine.

Keeping the tank clean

Tarantulas are not dirty animals. They produce only small amounts of white, powdery faeces, so their tanks do not need to be cleaned out very often. However, make sure you clean away food remains regularly, and wash out and refill the water dish every few days. Clean the sides and cover once every few months to keep the tank clean. Check first that any cleaning product you use is not harmful to your pet.

Temporary home

When you wash out the tank or change the substrate, you should always place your tarantula in a temporary plastic or glass container so that it cannot escape or get covered in cleaner.

Good conditions

If the tank is looking clean and not too damp, you can change the substrate just once a year. But if the substrate becomes waterlogged or mouldy, you should change it straight away. Remember to keep the tank well ventilated to prevent the build up of mould and fungi. These will give parasites such as mites somewhere to multiply.

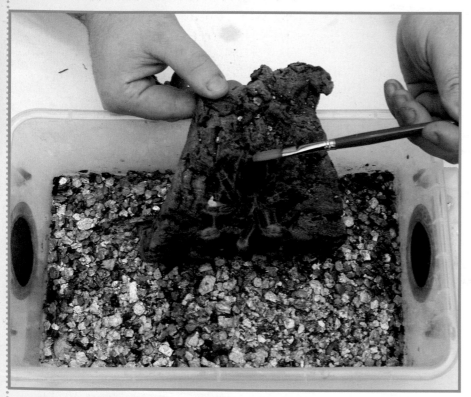

Use a soft paintbrush to gently persuade your spider to move to another container when you clean out its tank.

Moulting

In order to grow, a tarantula has to shed its hard outer skin. Adult tarantulas moult, or shed, their skins about once a year. When they are young they moult more frequently, while old tarantulas moult less often. When a tarantula is about to moult, it retreats to its shelter and seals itself in with a wall of substrate or silk. It usually lies on its back or side. Don't be tempted to disturb it at this time or you may kill it.

Tarantulas shed their skin in one piece. It takes about 24 hours for an adult spider to moult, and a few hours for a spiderling. You should not disturb or attempt to feed your tarantula for another week until its new skin has hardened slightly.

This tarantula moult contains all of its hard outer skin, including its fangs!

Ready to shed

If your tarantula's abdomen turns dark, it is probably a sign that your spider is about to moult.

Questions & Answers

✳ What if there is mould or fungi in the tank?
Clean out the tank thoroughly with mild disinfectant and rinse it with water. Change the substrate. Increase the air flow in the tank and keep the tank dryer for a while.

✳ What should I do if my tarantula gets an infestation of mites?
Mites can infest a spider as well as a tank. Clean out the tank and keep it dryer for a while (but keep the water dish in place), as mites do not like dry conditions. Seek medical advice from an expert or vet on how to treat your pet if it is badly infested.

✳ Why are tarantulas more vulnerable when they are moulting?
After moulting, a spider's new skin is soft and easily broken until it hardens up after a couple of weeks. Moulting is also very tiring and potentially dangerous for a spider (see page 27).

Handling your spider

When you get your spider, you may be very keen to pick it up to see what it feels like and how it moves. But you should remember that tarantulas are very fragile animals that can be seriously injured if they fall.

Fragile pets

Do not be tempted to pick up your tarantula too often. If you lose your grip or become frightened and drop your pet it could kill it, as their abdomens are very soft and are easily split. A tarantula finds being handled stressful – it may think you are picking it up to do it harm – and will bite you if it feels frightened. Never play with your spider and don't feel under pressure to show it off to your friends.

Let your tarantula wander on to your hand when it is ready to be held and provide it with plenty of support.

Moving your pet

The safest way to move a tarantula is to coax it into a jar or box without picking it up. You can encourage it to move forward by gently touching the spider's rear legs with a stick or soft paintbrush (see page 20). Once the spider is in the jar or box you can put a secure lid in place.

Spider proof!

Before you move your pet, it is worth making sure there aren't any holes in the room that your tarantula could squeeze into, just in case it does manage to escape. Close off any gaps and make sure you remove any sharp objects that could injure your pet.

Be patient

Take your time to get to know your spider before trying to move or handle it, and wait until you feel confident. If you put your hand into the tank and wave it around slowly you can see how your pet responds. You can then try gently stroking it with a brush or pencil. If it sends out defensive signals, such as rearing up the front of its body or rubbing off the hairs on its abdomen, then stay away.

If your spider remains calm, then you can try to encourage it to move onto your outstretched palm. Always have an adult with you when you do this. Do not let it wander on to your clothes as its tiny claws may get stuck in your clothes and be very difficult to disentangle.

Fear of heights

Do not pick your spider up more than a foot above a surface and do not hold it while standing up.

Emergency hold

On the rare occasion when you need to pick up your spider quickly, there is a correct way of holding it. Never pick it up by the abdomen or scoop the spider up in your hands. Pick it up gently by the cephalothorax, between the second and third pairs of legs. Get an adult to help you to do this.

The safest way to hold a spider is between its second and third pairs of legs. Don't squeeze too hard!

Questions & Answers

✴ **Is it hyglenic to touch my spider?**
You are unlikely to catch any nasty germs from touching your pet, but you should wash your hands after touching it to get rid of any hairs from the spider that may irritate your skin and cause a rash.

✴ **Will my spider bite?**
It shouldn't bite if you are gentle with it, but occasionally it might if it is frightened. Never attempt to pick up a spider while it is in its burrow or is moulting.

✴ **How can I capture a spider on the run?**
Have a fishing net handy so you can gently scoop your spider up and put it back safely in its tank.

Spider defences

Sometimes tarantulas may react in an unexpected way if they feel threatened. Look out for the warning signs and know what to do if you receive a nip.

Defensive measures

The first thing that a tarantula will do if it feels threatened is retreat and hide. If that isn't possible or it doesn't deter an attacker then it will 'kick' off hairs from its abdomen with its back legs. The hairs of some tarantulas have sharp tips that can be painful if they come into contact with your skin, eyes or throat (see page 10).

Why spiders bite

Almost all spiders are venomous and bite either to kill their prey or deter an attacker. Therefore a tarantula will only bite you if it feels frightened. That is why it is important to treat your spider with respect and don't disturb it too often or overhandle it. A tarantula can be very quick to strike.

This Goliath bird eating tarantula has developed a bald patch on its abdomen from flicking off its urticating hairs.

Irritating rashes

It is best to leave a spider alone if it starts to kick hairs. You may also need to take extra care when you clean out the tank as these hairs can come loose. Always see a doctor if a rash or irritation doesn't go away after a few hours.

Strike position

A tarantula's final defensive move is to rear back on its two pairs of back legs and expose its fangs. If this doesn't force the intruder to retreat, then the spider's next move will be to bite with its fangs. A tarantula bite is not lethal to humans – its effects are similar to a bee sting.

If you are unlucky and you get bitten, wash your bite wounds thoroughly and apply some antiseptic ointment. Then visit a doctor for a check up. Occasionally people can experience an allergic reaction to bites, which can make the symptoms much worse, so always seek medical advice if you have been bitten just to make sure you're okay.

A spider shows its fangs in its strike position.

Questions & Answers

* **Which tarantulas are the most dangerous?**
  Always avoid tarantulas from the Pterinochilus and Poecilotheria species as the venom in these spiders' bites can cause very unpleasant symptoms.

Warning!

If you experience vomiting or have difficulty breathing after your spider has bitten you, see a doctor immediately. You may be having an allergic reaction.

25

Signs of sickness

Tarantulas fortunately do not suffer from too many illnesses. Even so, you should be alert to signs of sickness that could affect your pet. Here are some common problems to be aware of.

Tank temperature

Tarantulas are fairly inactive so it may take time to notice something is wrong. If your spider has not eaten for three or four weeks and is showing no signs of moulting, then check the temperature of the tank. A tank that is too hot or cold may make your spider lose its appetite. Tarantulas, however, can be erratic in their eating habits without necessarily coming to any harm. Offer your spider a change in diet to try to get it to eat.

Mites

Watch out for parasites such as mites crawling on the substrate or spider. The best way to avoid a mite problem is to keep the tank very clean and avoid getting the whole area too damp (see page 20).

Remember to check your tarantula for signs of ill-health from time to time.

Dehydration

Always keep the water bowl topped up with clean water. A tarantula with a shrivelled abdomen is a sign that your spider has not had enough to drink, and can cause serious moulting problems. Provide it with plenty of drinking water and spray the tank regularly.

Moulting, cuts and wounds

If the tank is too dry during moulting, your spider's old skin might get stuck to the new skin in a few places and fail to shed. You can assist your spider by dabbing the affected area with water, or by gently using forceps to pull the old skin away. Get an adult to help you with this.

There is also a chance your spider's new skin may rupture before it has had time to harden. In this case your pet may lose lots of blood. Small wounds can be sealed with nail hardener, but large wounds, such as those caused by a fall, can sadly be fatal.

Sworn enemies

The tarantula's most dangerous predator in the wild is the Tarantula Hawk, a large wasp with a vicious sting.

Questions & Answers

✴ **Is something wrong if my spider has a bald patch on its abdomen?**

If your spider has a bald patch on its abdomen it's normal – it's just where it has been rubbing off its hairs. However, if your spider is rubbing off hairs a lot, it may be a sign that your spider is stressed and you should check that it is getting the care it needs.

✴ **What if my tarantula loses a leg in an accident?**

Spiders are able to grow back their legs automatically. Special muscles in the spider's body close off the leg stump, stopping bleeding, and a new leg emerges in the next shed.

Medical advice

It is a good idea to seek out a vet that has knowledge of tarantula treatment as soon as you get your spider, so you know where to take it if your spider becomes ill. Most vets should be able to give you a few helpful suggestions as to how to remedy illnesses or what to do in emergencies. You can also get in touch with your national tarantula society for advice on treating your pet.

This spider has grown new legs after an accident. Note how the new legs (the back two on the left) are thinner than the spider's others.

A spider's life

If you look after your spider well, it may live for ten or more years. During this time you will develop a strong bond with your spider.

Keep a record

Tarantulas can live for longer than you might think. Some female tarantulas can live more than 20 years. Why not keep a record of your spider's life with photos and pictures to remember it by? You could include photographs of your tarantula and tips on how to care for tarantulas, as well as information on all sorts of other spiders in the wild. It will be an important record of your pet's well-being and interesting to look back on over the years.

Tarantulas make unusual and fascinating pets, and you may grow very attached to yours.

An old spider

Over time you will notice that not only will your spider get bigger, but its behaviour might change, too. As your spider gets older it may moult less regularly and it may lose more of the hairs on its body. Be sensitive to its old age, and do not disturb it too much. When your spider finally dies you will feel sad, but at least you will have made the most of your time together.

Accidents and illness

If you are unlucky and your spider dies in an accident or from illness, try not to blame yourself. The chances are there was nothing you or anyone else could have done to prevent it. You may feel angry or guilty, or feel that it was unfair. These are quite natural feelings of grief. Talk to people about how you feel – it usually helps. You will soon be able to think about your spider with positive memories.

Happy home

In the wild tarantulas prefer to live in the same burrow all their lives.

Questions & Answers

✳ **How can I tell if my tarantula has died?**
If your pet is huddled up, with all its legs tucked underneath it, then it is probably dead.

✳ **Where can I find out more about tarantulas and spiders generally?**
Visit your local library or bookshop to find lots of books on spiders. You can also visit the arachnid houses of zoos and nature centres, and get in touch with arachnid organisations (see page 31) if you want to see tarantulas, other spiders and scorpions in the flesh.

Remembering your spider

You may decide to bury your tarantula in your garden when it dies. (Remember to check first that you are allowed to bury pets in your area.) You might like to have a small memorial service with your family and close friends. This is a nice way of showing your love and respect for your old friend.

It can be comforting to bury your pet in your garden.

Glossary

abdomen
In spiders, the abdomen is the rear section of the body, where most of the organs are found. In humans, the abdomen is another name for the stomach.

arachnid
An animal with a body made up of two parts, four pairs of legs and an external skeleton (or exoskeleton) formed from hard skin.

breeder
A person or organisation that breeds a particular type of animal.

captive-bred
Bred and born into an environment controlled by humans; not living in the wild.

cold-blooded
Having a body whose temperature varies with the surroundings.

endangered
In danger of extinction or dying out.

faeces
Droppings.

fungi
Spore-producing organisms that grow on plants and decaying matter.

gland
An organ that controls substances in the blood.

habitat
A place where an animal or plant lives.

humidity
The level of moisture in the air.

leg span
The total distance from the spider's first left leg to its fourth right leg.

mite
A tiny arachnid that sucks the blood of other animals.

moult
To shed old skin so that new growth can take place.

nocturnal
Active at night.

parasite
A living thing that feeds off and causes harm to another living thing.

pesticide
A substance used to destroy harmful insects, usually on crops or plants.

species
A group of animals that have characteristics in common and can reproduce (breed) together.

spiderling
A baby spider.

substrate
A layer of material at the bottom of a tank to provide comfort and warmth.

urticating
Urticating means 'stinging'. Urticating hairs can cause irritation or a rash.

venomous
Capable of injecting venom.

ventilation
A flow of fresh air in a closed space.

Useful websites

If you want to learn more about types of spiders, buying spiders, looking after spiders, or if you would like to get involved in animal welfare, these are some helpful websites:

UNITED KINGDOM
The British Tarantula Society
The main tarantula organisation in the UK. It organises shows for exhibiting and buying and selling tarantulas, runs a question and answer chatroom, displays adverts and publishes information on tarantula care. It welcomes new members.
Website: www.thebts.co.uk

The British Arachnological Society
Dedicated to furthering education on spiders; publishes articles on all sorts of spiders and includes a FAQs page for the public.
Website: www.britishspiders.org.uk
Email: info@britishspiders.org.uk

The Royal Society for the Prevention of Cruelty to Animals
News articles, rehoming information and animal care advice.
Website: www.rspca.org.uk
Contact address:
Enquiries service, RSPCA,
Wilberforce Way, Southwater,
Horsham, West Susses RH13 9RS

AUSTRALIA
The Australian Tarantula Association
Organises conferences and forums, and publishes information on different species of tarantula. New members welcome.
Website: www.theata.org

UNITED STATES OF AMERICA
American Tarantula Society
Organisation dedicated to furthering education on tarantulas and other arachnids. Members can leave messages and advice on a message board. Offers free downloads on tarantula care and sells books and CDs.
Website: www.atshq.org

American Society for the Prevention of Cruelty to Animals
Features pet care advice and campaigns fighting against animal cruelty.
Website: www.aspca.org

INTERNATIONAL
People for the Ethical Treatment of Animals
The world's largest animal rights group. Contains information promoting the safety and responsible treatment of animals.
Website: www.peta.org

Note to parents and teachers:
Every effort has been made by the Publishers to ensure that these websites are suitable for children, that they are of the highest educational value, and that they contain no inappropriate or offensive material. However, because of the nature of the Internet, it is impossible to guarantee that the contents of these sites will not be altered. We strongly advise that Internet access is supervised by a responsible adult.

Index